BETHAN

BEYOND MERCY

Revealing the Lie of Abortion

The opinions expressed in this manuscript are solely the opinions of the author and do not represent the opinions or thoughts of the publisher. The author has represented and warranted full ownership and/or legal right to publish all the materials in this book.

Beyond Mercy
Revealing the Lie of Abortion
All Rights Reserved.
Copyright © 2013 Bethany Greenleaf-Perez
v2.0 r1.0

Cover Photo © 2013 JupiterImages Corporation. All rights reserved - used with permission.

This book may not be reproduced, transmitted, or stored in whole or in part by any means, including graphic, electronic, or mechanical without the express written consent of the publisher except in the case of brief quotations embodied in critical articles and reviews.

Outskirts Press, Inc.
http://www.outskirtspress.com

ISBN: 978-1-4787-1676-1

Outskirts Press and the "OP" logo are trademarks belonging to Outskirts Press, Inc.

PRINTED IN THE UNITED STATES OF AMERICA

Contents

Foreword i
The Lie 1
Compromise 3
Becoming the Victim 5
Anguish Unleashed 9
A Slow Road to Redemption 13
Face to Face Encounter 20
Postscript 27

Foreword

I want to deeply thank Sheri Rowe and Michele Silva, two spiritual giants for Christ, for their encouragement and support. For a while I did not want to write about this intimate encounter with God. What Jesus said to me was so personal, and I was afraid someone might exploit his precious words to me. However, I also longed to tell every post abortion-suffering woman what I was told by the Lord. I wanted them to be as free as I was. Slowly, God started placing a trust in me, and he pressed upon my heart to write about what I was shown. I never want to say no to God again, and this is why you are holding this book in your hands. If you have had an abortion, God wants to completely heal you and set you free. This book is for you.

The Lie

Believing the deception of having an abortion severely scared my life in ways I never knew were possible. For many years I lived with this deeply buried pain, and I couldn't even listen to other people talk about abortion. It made me so uncomfortable that I would excuse myself from the conversation, and leave the room. I would force myself not to think about my abortion, other peoples' abortions, or abortion in general. My guilt was so multi-layered that I couldn't even say the word abortion. Over the years, God began to heal me from this indescribable pain. But there was one night, as we sat face to face, when Jesus completely removed all the remaining sorrow. I did not believe it would ever be possible, but that night for the first time since the abortion, I was truly free. My heart was free, and I could actually feel real joy where death once reigned. God also wants to heal you, and heal the millions of other women around the world who have had abortions.

What Satan meant for evil, God will use for his good and perfect purpose. God will use our suffering to keep future abortions from happening. It isn't the knowledge of sin that heals our souls; it's the **unveiling** of how deeply God forgives that makes all things new again. We will know the truth, and the truth will set us free. This is how we truly overcome.

Compromise

Being raised Catholic, abortion was not something I ever considered an option while growing up. I was a staunch believer in the pro-life movement, and I couldn't understand how anyone could ever justify having an abortion.

I remember, as a teenager, how someone really close to me was contemplating having an abortion. At the last minute this person decided not to go through with it, and I was secretly relieved. Even though I saw a few of my friends go through teen pregnancy, and I witnessed how they struggled being so young and unprepared, I still never considered abortion an option.

However, not too many years later, I learned that unplanned pregnancy at any age leads people to make decisions they never thought they could.

After college someone very close to me ended up having two abortions. I was appalled, judgmental, and I looked down on this young woman. I remained her friend, but I sincerely thought less of her. How could a woman willingly abort her baby? Looking back, I can only imagine how my condescending perception must have saddened God's heart.

Becoming the Victim

It's easy to judge others when you don't have to walk in their shoes. We do it daily, consciously, and subconsciously. God tells us to judge not, least we are judged. **That doesn't mean we don't take a stand for what is right; it means we show others the same mercy that has been shown to us through Jesus.** We aren't qualified to do anything else. When we extend the mercy of Jesus, then we become qualified to judge righteously.

As with most people, my childhood was less than perfect. My mother suffered a stroke while pregnant with my younger brother. She survived, but the emotional, spiritual, and physical handicaps that resulted from her illness made our lives a bit of a challenge. My dad was a functional alcoholic, and he drank to cope with all the difficulties Satan threw into our home. As a result, I became the pleaser and the overachiever while growing up. Being this type of child seemed to bring the accolades I desperately needed.

While my mother was in the hospital, and my father was working out of town, I was molested by someone my father entrusted his children with. I didn't even understand what had happened to me until many years later, but I had deep rooted emotional damage that I covered up successfully (or so I thought) for many years.

After high school I attended a private art school for a while. I became disillusioned with what it offered, returned home, and later on that year attended a state university. There I learned to party and to escape from the emotions I never allowed to surface.

After graduation I moved to a small resort community with my college roommate. We found seasonal employment and a partying lifestyle. I did not attend church, and I hung out with people who were into drugs and the occult for the entire summer. Later that year I found a teaching job, but I returned to the resort town once summer vacation hit, and to my partying friends.

That same summer I fell in love with the man I believed I was going to marry, but that relationship almost emotionally and spiritually killed me.

This man was tall, handsome, and extremely funny. He could make me laugh no matter what was going on around me. I could share my whole heart with him, and he treated me like I was the only one in the whole world that mattered. The fact that we drank like fish, snorted cocaine, and he was separated from his wife didn't seem to register as blazing red flags that had the potential to destroy me. When you are not living the life God desires for you, the enemy can be very successful at distracting you from the truth. My main focus was how much I loved this man. I believed whatever he told me, and I believed I was the most important person in the world to him.

We eventually moved in together, and I began to plan what a wonderful life we were going to have. It was at this point when my entire young adult life began to unravel. Shortly after moving in together, I discovered that I had become pregnant. My whole world changed, and the man that I thought was the love of my life changed too. I was no longer the most important person in his world; I became last on his list. He even told me that he had decided to reconcile with his estranged wife. His words stabbed my heart completely through, and I believed I was completely alone.

Not only was my heart shattered, I had no one I could turn to. Once the man I loved had decided to reconcile with his wife, how I could have this baby without her finding out? It would only ruin her life

too. What would be the purpose? He didn't want me anymore; why devastate two lives?

I couldn't go to my parents. They always told everyone that I was the child that stayed out of trouble. How could I tell them I had made such a huge mistake? I was the overachiever that my father was so proud of. His nickname for me was "bright and shining star." I couldn't bear to not be called that anymore. How could I let him down when he believed in me like he did? Too many people expected me to be the kid that didn't make mistakes like this; I couldn't let them down. Being the good kid, the overachiever, was who I was; it's all I had.

I even rationalized that the partying I had been doing most likely had damaged the baby anyway, and I would probably miscarry.

Over the next few days, I finally talked myself into making this life scarring decision. No one forced me, but if I had known how the abortion would devastate me for the rest of my life, I never would have allowed it to happen. If someone had shared with me what abortion truly does to you, I would have figured out another way to deal with my situation.

Anguish Unleashed

I remember the fog of my thinking while the man who was no longer the love of my life drove me to the abortion facility. I remember signing in, and waiting to be called. I remember the nurse stroking my hand just before the procedure, and how she reassured me that everything would be fine. I remember the doctor being visibly annoyed with me as I cried the whole time through the ordeal. I remember how impersonal and cold everything felt, and how no one seemed to understand the silent screams being released inside me. I remember walking out of the medical building with my heart so broken I thought I was going to die. I remember not believing what I had just done. I remember believing that I was now a lesser person, someone with a hidden secret, and I didn't want to live. I remember every detail. I remember.

On the way home from the abortion our car smashed into another car from behind. I slid off the front seat, hit my head on the dashboard, and slumped onto the floor. I remember being dropped off miles from where I lived (as not to be caught by the newly reconciled wife) as I walked home alone. I remember hot tears streaming down my face as I trudged along the side of the road. All I could hear were the words . . . worthless, pathetic, dirty, ugly, and stupid. The enemy of my soul kept whispering in my ear, "Just look at yourself now." When I finally reached my place, I curled up on my bed, and hoped I would die.

The next morning came, and I lay motionless on my bed, not wanting to get up or go on. I finally dragged myself to the mirror, and was completely horrified by my reflection. I could barely recognize the woman staring back at me. My forehead was one massive bruise, and the windows to my soul were glazed over in a darkened sadness that deeply frightened me. There were cries of anguish forming in the back of my throat, and I found it difficult to breathe. I had never felt so defeated, so worthless, or so pathetic in all my life. I had become what I had said I always hated. I heard the words of the adversary say, "See, you're everything I have always said you were." I looked away and hung my head in shame.

One night shortly after the abortion, I got together with the father of my now aborted child. He didn't want to talk about how I was feeling, and I didn't want to hear about his life without me. So we drank away our conversation until we were both completely numb from the alcohol, and I wanted to go home. I had parked my car in a parking lot up on a hill that was about a five-minute walk from where we had been partying. He waited for me at the bottom of the hill, while I went to get my car. There was only one way out of the parking lot. I simply needed to back out of the parking space, and turn left out onto the street. However, in my alcohol fog, I put the car in drive and drove across a lawn and down over approximately an eight-foot embankment onto the street below. I should have continued going straight into a big plate glass window of a television store, but somehow my car turned around in mid air. I landed facing the direction traffic should go. I landed with an incredible thud that violently bounced my car up and down, and shook me sober. I sat there in my car completely stunned and shocked that I was alive. Seeing what had just happened, my ex-boyfriend ran over to the car and asked me what I was doing. He was in disbelief at what he had just witnessed. Not knowing what else to do, and shaking like a leaf, I drove home. I sat on my bed while going over in my mind what had just happened, but it overwhelmed my ability to understand. I should have been killed, but I was sitting there very much alive.

The next morning I discovered that I had a hole in my gas tank, but there was no other damage to my car. I walked to work following an inch wide gas trail all the way into town. It stopped right where I had landed in the street. I looked at the embankment, and at the plate glass window I should have crashed straight into. There was no way in the universe that my car should have been able to turn around in mid air . . . it defied the laws of physics . . . I should have been dead. I have not shared this story with many people, until now, because who would believe me? But now I don't care if people don't believe me. It happened. My defeated ugly life was spared, why? I felt that I deserved death. Some Christians say that when you step out from under God's covering, he can't protect you. All I know is that He did protect me, maybe for a time such as this. God sees past the present, and sees our future, and sometimes he rescues us when we don't deserve it. But, then again, wasn't that the whole purpose of the cross? Sometimes he delivers us from the enemy's plan, for no other reason than because He is God, and he can do whatever he wants. I'm just so thankful for the mercy poured out on me, and how he died for me while I was still such a deliberate sinner.

==For more than a year after the abortion, I suffered from severe anxiety attacks, self-hatred, and pain so deep within my soul that if I allowed myself to feel it fully, I was sure I would lose my mind. Abortion had secretly made me physically ill. For a while, I wouldn't permit myself to even think about the abortion. I actually pretended that it didn't happen, because I just couldn't face it.==

A Slow Road to Redemption

Finally, one afternoon, I walked into a church sanctuary and sat down. The church was completely empty, and I just sat there in the silence and confessed to God what I had done. I didn't allow myself to become emotional about it, or I wouldn't be able to get through it. I simply confessed my sin, and told God how sorry I was. I knew God could forgive me, but I still couldn't forgive myself. I couldn't share how I was feeling with anyone; no one could ever know.

Well into my adulthood, God begin to heal me from the deeply hidden pain of being molested as a child. He didn't take me into years of therapy; he simply reached into my understanding, and allowed me to see him as he hung on the cross. As I looked upon my sins being heaped upon him, and the effect of sin from others done to me being heaped upon on him . . . I could not deny his loving sacrifice. He gave me everything he had, including his own life, so I could live. Then he breathed the following words into my heart:

A Red Tear Fell (the blood of Christ)

The Ancient of Days
in His perfection
allowed free will
even that of evil
and Satan sought to devour me

Only Satan couldn't see from the aftermath
in the infinite eternal time line
believing his weapons
his violations upon my soul
caused damage beyond repair

But the Ancient of Days
saw into forever
He knew I would survive
He knew my scars
would be the evidence of evil's existence
never to be ignored, but battled

As the Lord turned His face
unable to bear witness
as evil harmed His child
a red tear fell
and landed on my pain
and kissed my spirit
and gave me strength
and goodness

and self honor

The Ancient of Days
so deeply understood
creating me
would be worth every tear
Knowing
I would not die from the battle
Seeing past the evil
declaring my worth

I clearly see the scars
placed upon my soul
I wear them as a badge of courage
and a spit in the enemy's eye

I am not destroyed!

Once God healed my heart from that deeply hidden memory, he began to work on my heart concerning the abortion. Even though I believed I was forgiven, I never felt I was forgiven.

For one thing, I didn't know how my child in Heaven could ever understand why I had done what I did. That bothered me most of all. What must my child think? How could my child ever believe my love? I rehearsed in my head what I would say when we met one day, but I could never truly find the words to

justify to my child what I had done. How would my child ever believe me?

Many years later, I forced myself to sit down and write a poem to my child.

Till I Come Home

One day I know, I'll see your face
when God calls me home to you
And forever you I will embrace
breathe you in, live in your space

I have never once not wanted you
but instead believed a lie
The moment you were gone from me
never-ending sadness now resides

Forgive me, please forgive me
How I long to change that day
Your memory never leaves me
unbearable pain forever stays

Some day we'll be together
You will see my soul
And know I have never once
not loved you
as God guards you till I come home

All this emotional and spiritual damage was incredibly hard to deal with on a daily basis; I simply lived my life pretending I was okay. The Lord brought people into my life through work and social occasions that spoke to me about God's love. This was many times annoying. I already knew about God's love; I grew up in church. I had all the head knowledge, felt His presence, but deep inside I believed God loved me less because of what I had done. I believed I was a disappointment to Him, unworthy and not to be trusted. And the church did nothing to alleviate my torture. Most people in the body of Christ have a heavy tongue when it comes to abortion. I was once one of those people; but God is having me speak out now. There was even a time when a woman who was my friend said that she couldn't wait until judgment day so all the women who had abortions and all the doctors who had performed them could see all the babies they aborted, and who these babies would have turned out to be. I was so stunned by her statement that I wanted to crawl in a hole and die. I knew if she ever found out that I had an abortion, she'd want me to go straight to hell. It was unbearable to hear how people in the church condemned people who had abortions. How could we ever tell anyone, seek counsel, or ask for help to heal? We had to remain hidden and ashamed. People in the church had reduced the size of the cross, and limited God's love. There was no healing to be found in the place where it was needed most of all.

The relationships I had after the abortion were unhealthy, and they didn't last. When I finally started dating the man who is now my husband, I was attending church on a semi-regular basis. I was trying to get back into a right relationship with God, but once again, deep down I still felt worthless, ugly, and with secrets no one could ever know. I knew God loved me, but I thought I had to be last on his list of children. And the church had encouraged me to believe this lie. I had many sins, and I had had an abortion. How could God ever trust me again?

It wasn't until I gave birth to my son that I had a deep and profound revelation of God's unconditional love for me. I truly believe God gave me my son as a gift, as proof, of his great unending love for me. From the moment I held my son in my arms, and looked at his precious little face, I truly understood unconditional love for the first time. God did trust me; he gave me this child that was filling up that empty pain I had resigned myself to live with. I knew there would never be anything this child could do that would ever make me stop loving him. I understood how God could still truly love me.

Every day my son is a reminder of how much God loves me. I touch his face, and breathe in the goodness of God. One day when my son was still just a baby, I cried out to God to penetrate his heart, and make him a mighty man of God. That cry came from the deepest place in my soul, as I told God I could never bear to be without this child in Heaven. God honored that heart's cry, and my son accepted the Lord at a very young age. When he was little he would say, "Mommy, tell me about God." We would be riding in the car, and out of the blue, he would say, "Mom, can we talk about God?" I would silently thank God for hearing my prayer.

My son always disliked being an only child. One day I thought I would be strong enough to tell him that he had a brother or sister in Heaven, but I was afraid to tell him. I didn't want his opinion of me to change. When I finally did get up the courage to tell him, his reaction was one of pure love. He put his head in my lap and made me promise that I would never go far away from God again. He was as concerned about losing me as I was about losing his love. His acceptance of my imperfection was, yet again, another example of perfect unconditional love.

Face to Face Encounter

For many years I felt that I was as healed *as I possibly could be* from the scars of having an abortion. I talked to women about how to heal from sexual abuse, and how to heal from the sin of having an abortion. I talked about how when God forgives us, He throws our sins into the depths of the sea, never to be remembered again. I quoted all the scriptures on forgiveness, and spoke about the completeness of the cross. In my head I believed every word, but in my heart, I just couldn't accept how it was possible for God to forget when it came to abortion. I accepted that God could forgive abortion, but how could he forget the abortion when the evidence of that sin resided with him in Heaven?

One night, a few years later, during a time of resting in the presence of the Lord, I was taken into an open vision. I have experienced visions before. They are almost like dreaming, but you are awake. This open vision was completely different than anything I had ever experienced before. It wasn't like a dream. Suddenly, I was in Heaven sitting beside Jesus in some kind of seat that was suspended in mid air. The sights and sounds of everything around me were completely real and tangible. Jesus and I were face to face, and I was in complete awe of who he was. I was in a completely different place than on Earth, and it was if time was standing still. When I looked into the eyes of Jesus I understood for the first time, *"There is no condemnation in Christ Jesus."* When he looked at me I felt completely known, completely accepted, and completely loved from the inside out. It was as if he knew all the questions in my heart, and he wanted to talk to me about them, but my deepest question was about abortion.

Jesus said. "What do you want to ask me?"

So, I asked Him why I didn't *FEEL* completely forgiven concerning the abortion.

He looked at me and said. "Because you still believe you have to pay for it."

I hung my head and said. "Yes."

Jesus then said. "If you give me that lie, I will give you something in return."

So, I reached into my heart and gave the lie to Jesus. I don't know how I did it. I just looked into who I was, and let Him take it.

Jesus looked at me so tenderly, and then he looked down into my arms. So I looked down too, and gasped. He had placed my aborted child (and I knew it was a boy) into my arms. I was holding my baby, and tears of joy filled every part of my body. My baby boy had thick black hair, and big chocolate eyes. He was staring back at me, and I can't ever remember being so happy. Many moments passed, and I finally looked back at Jesus, and dared to speak. His face was so gentle and knowing. I kept thinking how unbelievably kind he was. I know that sounds so odd, but it's hard to describe perfect love. For the first time in my life, I was experiencing perfect love, and it consumed me.

When I finally spoke again to Jesus, I said. "I can understand how You can forgive the sin of abortion, but how can You forget this sin when You have the reminder (this person who was aborted) here in Heaven with you?"

Jesus tenderly looked at me, and smiled at me like I was a little child who didn't understand. There was no condemnation, no frustration, only love, and a desire for me to understand.

Jesus spoke with the most beautiful gentleness and said. "When I forgive abortion, I no longer see a woman who aborted her baby. I only see a mother who is temporarily without her child."

I suddenly felt like a child who had just been told the greatest truth of all. Such humility and awe overwhelmed me. When Jesus forgives abortion, He no longer sees a forgiven woman on Earth and her aborted baby in Heaven. He only sees a perfect woman on Earth waiting to be with her child who is temporarily without her.

"Ohhhh." I said. "I didn't see. I didn't understand."

Jesus simply smiled and said. "I know."

I finally understood what Jesus meant when He said that He makes all things new again. **When He forgives sins, it's as if they never happened and the reality of what was changes to something new. When there is no sin, there is no sin effect.** I felt like a thousand lights had been turned on in my understanding.

Jesus then began to show me many other things in Heaven. I saw my son as a toddler, a young child, a teenager, and as a young man. I saw my other son standing with him side by side. They looked so perfect, so strong, and healthy.

Jesus turned to me and said. *"There are your two sons."*

I had a peace forming deep within my soul for the first time. I was so overjoyed to be able to see my first child in and out of time, because there was no time. He was full of joy and always happy. What a relief that was for me. I had often wondered if my child was thinking about why I had aborted him, and how he would accept me. So I asked Jesus these questions as I watched my child play.

"Can I tell him how much I love him, and that I always wanted him?"

Again, Jesus looked at me with such mercy and tenderness as He answered.

"Your child does not live in that reality. He doesn't live in the reality of abortion. That's not who he is. He lives in the pure reality that he is temporarily without the mother that loves him. That is all."

Again, complete humility and awe of God's holiness overtook me. **My child will never live in the reality of my sin.** I couldn't believe it; I was so happy that my heart wanted to soar. Jesus had taken what I had done, and completely changed it from beginning to end. My child lives in purity and complete freedom. **I was finally grasping the true power of the cross.** I walked over to my son, and he looked at me as if he and I knew each other already.

He smiled with complete acceptance and love and said. "Hello, Mommy."

I smiled back at him and time stood still. There is no time in Heaven. It's as if my child and I have already lived as mother and son, because of the eternal timeline. Now and eternity are somehow one. I don't understand it all, but it was so real.

"For now we see as in a mirror, darkly: but then we shall see face to face. Now I know in part, but then I shall know as I am known. 1 Corinthians 12:12

There were many other things that I saw during my open vision. Most of it was personal, and of no interest to anyone but me. The one thing that I felt compelled to do was to share what was revealed to me about abortion. I know there are millions of women who are in as much pain as I was because of abortion. Jesus wants you to be free, truly free, and he wants you to have a voice.

Condemnation and guilt were nailed to the cross, but when it comes to abortion, many of God's people have prolonged the suffering of this sin for many women. I believe this is why the Lord gave me this open vision. I was a prisoner of this sin in the church, and it's time for the Body of Christ to set the captives free.

Abortion is a terrible, horrible, lie that America and many other countries live in. We must speak up and tell the world how devastating abortion is, and about its demoralizing side effects that last a lifetime. It is the women who have lived in this lie that must be heard. We must speak now for each other, and for the unborn. We are the ones who can turn the hearts of the people. We are free; now what will we do with this freedom?

"Behold, I make all things new again." Revelation 21:5.

Postscript

Since writing "Beyond Mercy" I had another deeply hidden secret in my heart cleansed. Years ago I had a partial revelation of the cross when it came to being healed from the childhood memory of molestation. However, there was still hidden anger, fear, and bitterness when it came to the reality of an innocent child being scarred in this way. Recently, while praying, I dared to get completely vulnerable with the Lord about this being allowed to damage the innocence of my childhood. I needed more revelation to erase the secret anger, pain, and the fear. I was a little wisp of a thing who loved the Lord and all of his creation. My family was torn apart, evil stamped its ugly mark on me in place of my innocent intimacy, and killed what was to be an extension of perfection. It was allowed to happen; why? Why does evil get to harm innocent children? I can understand it having access to adults who sin or fall away from the love and protection of Father God, but not innocent children who are at the mercy of evil. Why? Why is that allowed? How are we, as children, ever to feel safe when we are not protected from this evil? How do we not live in fear when we have experienced not being protected? I understood how God is perfect love, and perfect love casts out all fear – but I was fearful. I needed to understand how to not wear this fear, instead of pretending it wasn't there. How do we trust that evil has no power when it did have power to scar me so deeply?

Suddenly, I was taken back to my childhood to the night it happened, but there was complete safety. As darkness entered the room and schemed to devour me, Jesus scooped me (my spirit) up and carried me to a place as high as the top of Redwood trees. As evil tried to overwhelm me, Jesus and I looked away. We cast our eyes out beyond the beauty of the atmosphere as we lingered in the peace of creation. We breathed in goodness, mercy, and perfect love. I heard the Lord say, **"This is where I was. I removed you, and we looked away, as I held you in my arms."**

I understood in completeness that we are only to be concerned with what can destroy us spiritually, not what can harm our bodies. The revelation we receive "by the renewing of our minds" through the Holy Spirit truly makes all things new again, and all things possible. My finite (incomplete) understanding gripped me with the limitations of anger, bitterness, and fear. But when Jesus showed me that at the very hour when I thought I was the most vulnerable and unprotected, **he was right there.** When Jesus said he will never leave us or forsake us, he was telling the truth. My human understanding did not comprehend what was happening in the spirit. He did not leave me alone to deal with evil . . . **He removed the part of me that could not be destroyed, and we looked away.**

We do not always see what is going on in the spirit realm as evil comes our way, but we must know, beyond our human comprehension, that we are never alone.

Matthew 28:20 "And surely I am with you always, to the very end of the age."

I wanted to share this latest understanding, because, as people in this fallen world, we suffer a great deal at the hands of evil. We must understand that the enemy of our souls wants us to believe that God does not love us enough to protect us. The enemy wants us to believe that God's love has self-preservation qualities, and He willingly limits his strength and covering over us. However, we must understand that GOD IS PERFECT LOVE. HE IS LOVE SO POWERFUL THAT HE CAN RAISE HIMSELF FROM THE DEAD. When He died in our place, we were given the very key to life itself.

CPSIA information can be obtained
at www.ICGtesting.com
Printed in the USA
BVHW07s0357270918
528627BV00001B/35/P